What Does A Jew Look Like?
by Keith Kahn-Harris and Robert Stothard

Published by Five Leaves Publications
14a Long Row, Nottingham NG1 2DH
fiveleaves.co.uk
fiveleavesbookshop.co.uk

Paperback ISBN 978-1-910170-84-7
Hardback ISBN 978-1-910170-87-8

Design and layout by Departures®
Printed in Great Britain

WHAT DOES A JEW LOOK LIKE?

Keith Kahn-Harris
Robert Stothard

Foreword by Stephen Bush

Foreword

Stephen Bush

I am the author of this book. I don't mean to say that I did any of the work, or the thinking, much less the writing, the organisation or the chivvying of writers and the gentle chiding about missed deadlines. Indeed, if I am being 100% honest, I have to admit that I myself added to some of that workload by missing my own deadline.

No, what I mean is: I am one of those awful journalists who has, in the past, illustrated a story about Jewish life in the United Kingdom with a picture of the Haredi community. I've made all the usual journalistic excuses: the desk wanted a picture, it's hard to illustrate abstract stories, it's harder still to illustrate stories about race or religion in a sensitive way, and so on. I've engaged in special pleading about the fact that, look, I'm Jewish, so of course I know that there's more to Jewish life in twenty-first century Britain than living in Stamford Hill. (I, for example, am barely observant and live a whole twenty minutes' walk away in Stoke Newington.)

These are poor excuses, not least because I've never hesitated to get annoyed when I see other journalists using the same old photo to illustrate a story about our community — even when it obviously doesn't fit. (I once saw a picture about Jewish schools illustrated with a picture of three Haredi men, all of whom were visibly over fifty.)

Of course, these are all bad arguments. The difficulty, we journalists like to explain, is that just as with, say, the care crisis, which isn't solely about the elderly, it's hard to illustrate the story without resorting to stereotype. Given that the one thing journalists like to do more than resort to easy cliché is to find an excuse to put a picture of a pretty young person in the paper, you'd think we'd leap at the chance to put a photo of our own choosing to illustrate a story about British Jewish life: yet we don't.

It's the ubiquity of the same old image to depict our community — in some cases, the same photo taken on the same day, pressed into service to illustrate stories on everything from literary prizes to street antisemitism to the ongoing problems in the Labour Party — that has inspired this collection.

And, as this collection illustrates, one reason why we shouldn't use this photograph is that, while our strictly Orthodox communities are a big (and, unless the next census springs a very big surprise, the fastest-growing) part of British Jewish life they aren't the only part. There's no reason why we shouldn't illustrate a story about British Jews with a picture of the traffic island at Golders Green, or a stunningly attractive young political journalist in the Stoke Newington area, for that matter. The story in these pages is of interesting, living and breathing people, with different ideas of what it is to be Jewish, with different journeys to feeling Jewish, who live in different parts of the United Kingdom and have very different lives. And they each deserve representation.

But the other reason is that, as this book also shows, everyone deserves to have their own story told. A Haredi man, young or old, deserves better than to be used as a journalistic crutch to illustrate each and every story about communal life. A picture may tell a thousand words, but as this collection shows, those thousand words aren't anywhere near as compelling as letting the subject speak, not on behalf of a whole community, but for themselves.

Introduction

Keith Kahn-Harris
What does a Jew look like?

It's easy to live one's entire life in Britain without encountering a real
live Jew. There are around 300,000 Jews living in this country — a fraction
of 1% of the population — and they are disproportionately clustered
in parts of London, Manchester, Leeds, Glasgow and a few other cities.
Even though some neighbourhoods have a reputation as being heavily
Jewish, Jews do not form a majority in any Parliamentary constituency
or local council.

Inevitably then, for most British people, their impression of who
Jews are will be heavily influenced by how Jews are *represented* publicly.
Also inevitably, that representation is partial, giving an incomplete picture
of British Jews. Publicly, we see and hear from and about Jews in a limited
number of ways in a limited number of contexts: In school curricula,
we find Jews practicing Jewish religious rites. In the news media, we find
Jews campaigning against antisemitism and Jews talking about Israel.
In public ceremonies we find Jews commemorating the Holocaust.
In entertainment media we find Jews cracking jokes.

In some ways, Jews in this country have never been more visible,
more spoken about and also more outspoken themselves. While the
controversy over antisemitism in the Labour Party has been the most
obvious manifestation of this, British Jews have become much more
assertive and visible in the public sphere since at least the early 1990s.
While some of that assertiveness has concerned antisemitism, we have
seen much more investment in and public celebration of Jewish life and
culture too.

And yet this greater visibility has, paradoxically, led to increasing
confusion about who Jews actually are. Part of this confusion arises from
the diversity of British Jewry and the range of their beliefs and practices.
This is connected to a wider confusion of where to *situate* Jews. Are Jews
a religion, an ethnicity, a nation or something else? Are Jews 'white'?
Are Jews Zionists? Are Jews rich? And what do we do with Jews who
are not part of the majority of British Jews or who do not fit into any
existing category?

These difficulties in knowing where to situate Jews reach their apotheosis in questions of *visibility*. The answer to the question 'What does a Jew look like?' frequently reveals all kinds of unacknowledged assumptions about who Jews are. And there is one particular image of Jews that embodies this...

Two black-hatted, black-coated, bearded men are walking down the street, one of them leaning slightly towards the other as if he is explaining something. We do not see their faces and their identity seems to be surrounded in mystery. Yet we do know this — they are the Jewiest of Jews.

This picture has now been used dozens, possibly hundreds of times in the British media to illustrate stories about Jews. Along with a few other similar photographs also showing black-hatted men with their backs to the camera, it has become *the* image of Jews in this country.

Such an image seems to answer the question 'what does a Jew look like?' with an unambiguous answer: Jews wear black hats, black coats and have beards; they are mysterious, perhaps secretive, and women are invisible. Such Jews have been made generic because they seem to be the 'most' Jewish. Jews that look 'just like us' or who signify in more ambivalent ways cannot stand for the whole. Only those who cannot be assimilated into 'us' can truly represent 'them'.

These are what are known as Haredi Jews (sometimes known as ultra-orthodox, sometimes known as Hassidic, although only one segment of this particular population actually identifies with this term). It isn't unreasonable that they should have a significant profile amongst British Jews. The Haredi Jewish population of Britain is growing fast, doubling every twenty years. And yes, the men do generally wear black hats, black coats and have beards.

When images of Haredi Jews are treated as images of generic Jews, the considerable differences between their own and other Jewish communities are elided. For example, I once saw a newspaper article about antisemitism at Oxford University illustrated with one such image, even though only a tiny minority of Haredim attend university. Although there is a fair amount of crossover, the needs and concerns of Haredi Jews and other Jews are often very different. The fast-growing Haredi community in Stamford Hill, for example, is made up of very large families and faces considerable pressure on housing, something that doesn't apply in the same way to the Jewish community in Radlett.

Some Haredi Jews might be pleased to be thought of as the epitome of authentic Jewishness. Yet treating them as generic also overrides the diversity of their own community. There is no one Haredi Jewish community, rather there is a kaleidoscopic collection of sects and communities. Indeed, while to the outside the men might all look the same, there are many subtle distinctions in how they dress that are highly meaningful to insiders. Further, Haredi women are neither entirely invisible nor without agency; many work and some have significant leadership positions within some communal institutions.

The ubiquitous use of stock photos is a relatively recent phenomenon. There was a time when most newspaper stories were not illustrated and those that were drew on specially commissioned photographs. As printing and design technology was revolutionised from the 1980s onwards, so a broader range of illustrations became possible. When newspapers began to be published online as well as in print, each story was required to have an illustration. With the need to publish online as fast as possible, editorial staff have had to draw on sources other than specially commissioned photographs in order find appropriate images — with little time to reflect on their choice.

In seeking to understand how stock photos of Jews are produced and reused, I traced the most famous one of all back to its origins. The image of two Haredi Jews walking away from the camera is available on Getty Images, one of the largest photo libraries, from which images are downloadable and reusable for a fee or by subscription. That one particular photograph was part of a set, originally produced to illustrate a story that actually was about Haredi Jews in Stamford Hill. Many pictures from the set have never been used. The images that pictured Haredim from the front do not seem to have been used to illustrate newspaper stories; indeed, there are photos showing the faces of the two men in the famous photo that have never been used. Clearly, there is something attractive about the faceless Haredi Jew.

Of course, it is easy to complain about the use and reuse of generic stock photographs of Haredi Jews. It is much more difficult to suggest alternatives. How is a hard-pressed editor supposed to find a picture that says 'Jew' with fifteen minutes notice?

If there is a solution, it doesn't just lie in the newsroom itself. Rather, the root of the problem is that the confusion over who Jews are is such that the only consensus answer to the question 'What does a Jew look like?' is 'A Haredi Jew'. Editors have to choose the image that signifies most strongly, and nothing signifies as strongly as black hats, black coats and beards.

The challenge, therefore, is to help those who are not Jewish (and even some who are) to understand the diversity of Jews. The question of who Jews are and what they look like cannot be cleared up; it is intrinsically complicated. Non-Jews need to reconcile themselves to the fact that that Jews can be many things. If that fact was widely acknowledged, then a much broader range of images would signify as Jewish. While no one image can stand for the whole, that would matter less if the necessarily partial nature of individual images were recognised as just that. It wouldn't be a problem to illustrate one story about all Jews with a picture of Haredi Jews, so long as other stories were illustrated with a range of other pictures of other kinds of Jews.

This book offers a modest contribution to this project. It will offer a range of answers to the question 'What does a Jew look like?' in order to demonstrate that there can never be one generic Jew.

The book is the result of a collaboration between the photographer Rob Stothard and me. I first contacted Rob (who is not Jewish) in 2018 when I saw that he was the one who had taken that set of photos in the Getty Images archive. Rob was also uncomfortable with the way in which his photos had become ubiquitous and decontextualised. He certainly had never set out to photograph the generic Jew.

Rob and I decided to work together to produce some different images of British Jews. In this collaboration there was a clear division of labour: I used my knowledge of British Jewry to select subjects and Rob worked with them to produce an image that was both aesthetically pleasing and an expression of who they understood themselves to be, Jewishly and otherwise. Rob came to this project with no agenda other than an artistic one. He listened and learned about the diversity of Jewish life while being responsive to the individual idiosyncrasies of his subjects.

There are many ways of presenting portraits. One of the key decisions we had to make was how much contextual information we should include in the book. In 2019–2020, the Jewish Museum in London exhibited a collection of photographs by John Offenbach called simply *Jew*. Like us, John was keen to demonstrate Jewish diversity (in his case worldwide, rather than just in Britain) and his portraits represent many different faces of Jewish life. All the portraits were taken against the same background and he provided virtually no contextual information, giving only a name, location and profession. John's work was designed to provoke questions about what makes Jews distinct. In many cases, the viewer is forced to ask, 'If I didn't already know this person was a Jew, how would I know? And why might it matter anyway?'.

The approach we took in this book is the reverse of Offenbach's. Whilst both projects are concerned with Jewish diversity, in our project we embed the images of their bodies and faces in context. Rob worked closely with all the subjects to find a location that was meaningful to them, sometimes highlighting objects that are of particular significance. Further, each picture is accompanied by the subject's own words, either written by them or obtained by interview.

One of the consequences of this contextual approach is that it makes it deliberately difficult to see the subjects as 'representatives' of a particular way of being Jewish.

When I began to seek out subjects for Rob to photograph, I identified particular types of Jew that I wanted to include in the book: Haredi, modern orthodox, progressive; old and young; male, female and non-binary; cisgender and transgender; Zionist and non-Zionist; left-wing and right-wing; from London and from the rest of the country; Ashkenazi, Sephardi, Mizrachi and other ethnicities; and so on. However, as the project progressed it became increasingly clear that we would inevitably have to end up leaving out some particular demographics. That was, in part, because the photo sessions took much more time to set up than we had anticipated.

It was also because only a book of hundreds of photographs could adequately represent the many sub-groups that British Jewry includes. So readers may well be as interested in who *isn't* in the book as who is.

These limitations notwithstanding, the collection of portraits in this book still includes a wide variety of Jews. It includes people who are associated with some of the different factions and points of view in the sometimes bitter political conflicts that occur within the Jewish community itself. In addition, some of those included in the collection might not be considered as Jewish at all according to some definitions of Jewish law. This collection does not take a position on these highly sensitive issues. The book seeks only to represent the diversity of those who define themselves as Jewish. We do acknowledge though, that some of those included in the book may find their proximity in its pages to other sorts of Jews a little challenging.

By placing the subjects in their preferred context and by allowing them to define their Jewish lives in their own terms, they cease being representatives of anything but themselves. They become Jewish people, not generic Jews. Even when we deliberately chose subjects in order to ensure a particular slice of British Jewry was represented, the subjects themselves ended up undermining our pretentions. In several cases, the reason we actually chose a subject ended up being almost entirely absent from their account of themselves.

The portraits, while they may have been composed by Rob and their subjects with enormous care and attention, are brief snapshots of the subjects' lives at a particular point in time. The project took longer than expected as it was interrupted by the Covid-19 pandemic and in some cases, the subjects have moved house, moved jobs or moved onto another stage in their lives since the photographs were taken. They remain Jews.

So what does a Jew look like?

It's a crude question. While not antisemitic in and of itself, it's certainly the sort of question that someone who is hostile to Jews might ask. Indeed, one of the subjects in the book has deep misgivings about the title of this book. Yet it's also important to acknowledge that the question might be asked in good faith, perhaps by an editor who is pressed for time, or by someone who genuinely knows no better.

Hopefully, the reader of this book will learn that to find the answer to this question they must engage in a process rather than locate a particular image. If you want to discover who British Jews are, the best way to do so is to observe, listen and find the humanity in each one. To understand what a Jew looks like, accept what you do not know and revel in the insolubility of the individual puzzles that each Jew represents.

How to find out more

The self-descriptions of each of the subjects in this book frequently make use of Jewish terms and refer to Jewish organisations and practices. These are listed and explained in the glossary at the end.

For a fuller explanation of the various UK Jewish denominations, organisations and communal bodies, see Keith Kahn-Harris's factsheet 'Branches of Judaism', published by the Religion Media Centre at www.religionmediacentre.org.uk/factsheets/branches-of-judaism. The same website also has factsheets available on other aspects of Judaism.

Acknowledgements

Rob Stothard and Keith Kahn-Harris would like to thank the Bridging Trust, The Shoresh Trust and the Rifkind Levy Charitable Statement for their support for this project.

We are grateful to all of those who appear in this book for their time and patience. We would also like to thank all those who put us in touch with potential subjects. In particular, Anita Fox was enormously helpful in facilitating our prison visit.

WHAT DOES A JEW LOOK LIKE?

The photo was taken in my grandma's house, where I live now. I always trusted her and felt connected to her. The kitchen was the centre of her home.

When I was younger, my parents made *aliyah* and I came back to the UK. I was subsequently sexually abused in the family home that I lived in. It started off that I was coming to my grandma's for her to look after me but it very quickly turned into me looking after her. We very much looked after each other.

I didn't disclose the abuse to her at the time. But I did disclose it to her later, when she was well into her 80s. In the same conversation she told me that she had been sexually abused as an eleven-year-old girl and she'd never ever disclosed this before.

My life moved on and I got married and had three children. My grandma died about eight years ago. The house was rented out. When things reached boiling point and I needed to leave my husband, it just so happened — and I don't believe in coincidences — that the tenant gave a week's notice to leave. So within a week I had packed my stuff and my children and I was lucky enough to be able to move in here.

This house is the first place I could be independent and live for myself. I got married when I was eighteen and started to have babies very quickly after that.

I come from a *Litvish* background. I don't think Haredi is a helpful term. Internally we don't call ourselves Haredi. We say things are *heimishe* or *frum*. I am all of those things.

I haven't left the community. Why should I have to leave the community to have autonomy? I'm here and I'm staying. My children go to schools within the community and I have lots of friends.

My staying has led to some uncomfortable conversations and yes, it is painful at times. Me being here and talking publicly about what I experienced forces people to confront problems within the community.

Mine is an unusual story. Most people present it as a binary choice: either stay and abide by community norms or leave. Why do people have to be so binary?

This photo was taken at the soundcheck to my band 1919's gig at the Dublin Castle in Camden. I became something of a rebel in my teenage years and was drawn to punk and metal, and though the former has made more of a lasting impact in my creative output, there was a special importance for some bands in the latter category: KISS, Twisted Sister... Not only larger than life, but they looked like me too.

I grew up about as oblivious to Judaism as was possible with a name like Goldhammer. I attended the nearest primary school to where I lived as a child, a C of E school round the corner from my grandfather's house in North Yorkshire. He was a Polish Jew born in 1933. As my brother and I were from a family where my mother was the lone parent, my grandfather was the main patriarchal figure.

There were few reminders of our heritage in our day-to-day lives bar the Chanukah cards we opened alongside our Christmas ones. Adolescence changed that though. Keen for us to learn of our history, our mother took us, at twelve and thirteen, to Auschwitz during the school holidays. We'd started to cover WWII, Anne Frank and the *Shoah* at school, and my grandfather would start to open up to my brother and me in a way he'd never done with his daughter. Siberia had been his fate as a boy, not Oświęcim. Hardly a consolation prize but ultimately the difference between survival and not (his parents weren't so lucky though).

As if I needed a constant reminder of my place in all of this, puberty had gifted me a nose that it would take six years to grow into. With the dawn of social media a few years later, my family name would also accompany me in any encounter I would have. It's little wonder then, that my sense of Jewishness grew stronger as the years went by.

One by one, over the years, we lost my grandfather and all but one of his generation. During that time my mother had also started to work with her local (Orthodox) synagogue, recruiting help from her sons whenever there was furniture to be moved. Consequently, I've probably spent more time in a synagogue than generations of my family ever did. The community has been there for my mother in times of emotional hardship in recent years.

I lit a *menorah* at home for the first time this year, despite still being totally irreligious, and was moved significantly by the experience. After all, a lack of faith made no difference to the Gestapo or the KGB...

I grew up in the Swiss Alps. On my parents' farmland we have a certain type of very sturdy tree called a stone pine. These grow at a great altitude and under the most difficult climatic conditions.

A well-known philosopher once took notice of this special tree in a valley just next to where I grew up and used it as a metaphor for strong and independent human willpower. When we were harvesting some of these trees, I thought it would be befitting to shape a *shtaender* (Yiddish for 'lectern') out of its wood, to take up the philosopher's metaphor and make it subservient to the great ethical values and moral obligations of our Torah. Henceforth, the stone pine would hold prayerbooks, Talmud volumes and Torah-related literature. The aim, to shape the one who sits behind these books with G-d's help into a real *mensch*. Not willpower for its own sake which is dangerous, but a strong and independent commitment to be able to serve humanity, being beneficial to society and the world should be the transformative power and driving force of my project.

For me, the acquisition of knowledge of our great tradition must be in balance with what I practice in my daily life, how I interact with others, with the world around me, how this knowledge fosters good character traits.

Quite a number of happy circumstances have brought me from a farmer's family in the Swiss Alps to the rabbinate of an open-minded, warm-hearted Orthodox community here in Kingston-upon-Thames. Both university studies and years of first-hand experience at the side of one of the most outstanding rabbinic scholars of contemporary Orthodox Hassidism have shaped my deliberate choice of rabbinic leadership style: it is the one commonly described as 'the middle path'. Even though this way of living one's Judaism has been belittled in the often-repeated quote that 'only a horse walks in the middle of the way,' I think this is a great misunderstanding and caused much damage and unfortunate polarisation within a minority that cannot afford further splits if it is to survive.

Living open-minded and engaged in the wider society while at the same time being absolutely committed to our tradition and Jewish Orthodox law is not a compromise, but the most challenging way of being Jewish, and for me personally the most inspiring one.

I was born and grew up in Brighton. My family was always involved with the community and we were active members of an Orthodox *shul*. I still go there occasionally, more out of a sense of familiarity than anything else.

I went to Israel when I was seventeen as part of the *Machon* programme. The idea was to spend a year in Israel studying followed by time on kibbutz. Afterwards we were supposed to return to the UK to work in the youth movements. I was a huge failure as I fell in love with Israel and stayed for four years.

From Jerusalem I went to New York and worked for the Conference of Presidents of Major American Jewish Organisations for six years. That taught me everything I needed to know about politics, diplomacy, high stress and how to deal with lots of egos! I worked there through Operation Solomon (the airlift of the Ethiopian Jewry to Israel), the first Gulf War, the opening of relations between Israel and the Palestinians and the fall of the Berlin wall.

I met my husband in New York and then we returned to Israel to start raising a family. We were in Jerusalem for nearly four years but after Rabin was assassinated everything changed, there was a loss of hope and an increase in terrorism. With two young children it became too oppressive, so we returned to Brighton.

Wherever I have lived, being Jewish has been an integral part of who I am. It's not something I've ever tried to hide or deny. Moving back to Brighton forced me to be a more public Jew, speaking out against the virulent anti-Israel behaviour I saw in the city. I was a founder member of Sussex Friends of Israel, which was an opportunity for Jews to lift their heads above the parapet, to be loud and proud of their Jewish identity instead of the old 'stay quiet, don't make a fuss' mentality.

I will always defend Israel's right to exist. As I have always supported Palestinian rights, I find it hard to understand why so many people think that it has to be one or the other — for me they sit comfortably side by side.

More recently I have become a spokesperson for Labour Against Antisemitism. A different role as I'm more used to working behind the scenes and not being so public. But if it helps in the fight against antisemitism then so be it.

Kenneth

Sheffield

The photo was taken in Norfolk Heritage Park, Sheffield. That's the place I usually walk on Shabbat. I've had a relationship with trees since I was a child. I've lived in Sheffield for over four years now, after moving from London, where I was born and raised. I came to Sheffield to get away from the London anxiety!

I'm a member of the Seven Hills Synagogue. It's small, maybe 100 people, so it's a very tight-knit and friendly community. We don't have our own building, so we meet in a community centre every other week.

I'm part of a sub-group here where we build up diversity and inclusivity within the Jewish community, trying to engage with our members to talk about the presence of Disabled Jews, Black Jews, Jews of Colour and Queer Jews. It's a way to help them adapt within those spaces through social activities and promote an accepting diversity of Jews everywhere.

My parents are Nigerian Igbos. They moved to the UK in the 1980s but divorced in the early 2000s. Though my Mum is Christian, some reputable anthropologists believe in the theory that Igbos have Hebrew Israelite origins.

Ironically, I first heard about Judaism through my childhood learning difficulties when I was seven years old. I went to a secular school in the Jewish Haredi neighbourhood of Stamford Hill. I had a teaching assistant who was a secular Jew, and I asked her questions whenever we went to the library nearby. For example, once I asked, 'Why are these people dressed like that?' She told me there are strictly practising Jews and explained the different movements of Judaism.

I embraced Judaism in the early 2010s as I love the idea of *tikkun olam*, being spiritually conscious, doing *tzedakah*, and celebrating my ancestors contribution to the Torah. I want to build consciousness of overseas Afro-Caribbean Jewish communities in the UK to advocate for their recognition within Jewish Education.

There are other Black Jews with Afro-Caribbean heritage in cities like London, Birmingham and Manchester. The problematic issue in Jewish spaces is explaining the connections between African ethnic groups and the biblical tribe of Israel; people get confused, and I constantly have to explain. Not only ethnic groups such as the Igbo, the Akan, the Lemba, and the Abayudaya — but other African Jewish communities make the same claim.

I'm immensely proud of the fact that The Beatles, The Rolling Stones, The Clash and The Sex Pistols, were all managed by Jews. I think it says a lot about us. Brian Epstein, Andrew Loog Oldham, Malcolm McLaren and Bernie Rhodes all had the courage, the imagination and the chutzpah to upset and redefine popular culture in much the same way that Jews have done in politics, science, medicine, psychotherapy and comedy in the last century or so. Usually while being persecuted. I like to think revolution runs in our DNA.

Our family makes Shabbat dinner every Friday. We all wear hats, mine's an old British pith helmet I bought in Jaffa 30 years ago. We have a good sing song round the table and even the cats get a 'big up' in the opening number. When I blow out the candles just before going to bed, I hold Mum's silver candlesticks in my hands, shut my eyes and feel her close by.

My first real experience of performing on a 'stage' was at Wembley Orthodox Synagogue in January 1978, singing from the Torah on the day of my *bar mitzvah*. I sang in the *shul* choir and was once asked by our wonderful *chazan* to do a duet with him during *Kol Nidre*. That was pretty big news back then and my dad still talks about it as if it was yesterday. When I was doing a play at the National Theatre a few years ago, I warmed up before every show singing that song. When the Prodigy's sound system broke down mid-set at Glastonbury back in 1997, I was asked to go on stage and keep the frustrated crowd at bay whilst they tried to fix it. I didn't have any jokes and was getting bottles thrown at me, so I decided to sing *Hava Nagila* to 92,000 people and thankfully it worked a treat. That song really saved my arse that night.

I visited Auschwitz about ten years ago, it was in the winter and there were very few people around. As night fell and I made my way to the exit, I got into a conversation with a man who wasn't Jewish and at one point he asked me if I had any children. I told him that I had three, when in fact I only have two. I've never in my life lied about how many kids I have. Somewhere deep inside me, I guess that two children just hadn't felt like enough to defiantly state that we'd survived.

I am a practising artist — concentrating on drawing and installation, my work explores themes of identity, memory, sexual violence, and the body. Largely autobiographical, I use biological materials such as broken eggshells and living matter — plants, insects, fungus — as media, either drawing directly onto them or using them to transform objects and spaces.

I was brought up with a very strong religious and cultural identity, but in a non-traditional household. Our family was part of the radical feminist movement; I was conceived through donor insemination and the household was very much part of that 1980s leftist Stoke Newington scene. There was always a degree of balancing political and personal ideology with religious practice. To make keeping kosher dietary laws easier, we were vegetarian. I went to a Jewish primary school. We'd go on Friday to Ridley Road market to buy *challah*, and we lit candles and had traditional Friday night dinner to welcome in Shabbat, when I wasn't allowed to turn on the TV or touch anything electric. As I got older and my mum left the more radical circles, we became more traditionally observant and moved to a more Jewish area of London. I studied in seminary for two years pre-university and got married whilst a student to my long-term boyfriend.

As an adult, I have moved back to East London and now live with my husband in Bow. I have a studio in Woolwich where I work and can plan projects. I lived in Edgware for many years but felt stifled and constrained by the atmosphere there — the main thing I miss about it is the excellent foraging in the local woodlands! Living away from the North West London Jewish bubble allows me more freedom to be religious and observant but also to lead a more unconventional life without the scrutiny or pressure of a curious and conservative community. I do not currently want children so many of the tropes of religious married life do not fit my own. I can cover my hair, keep kosher, go to *shul*, go to the *mikvah* and fulfil *mitzvot* without having to live in a row of houses all of which have *mezuzot*.

Growing up, my family weren't members of a synagogue or in any way involved with the Jewish community so I had no Jewish connections as a young person. I was born in Edinburgh where I lived until the age of twenty-two, until moving to Lochmaben in Dumfriesshire where, having married at the age of twenty, I became almost completely occupied with having a family of five children! I did find time on a part-time basis to be a playgroup leader, a swimming instructor, a maths tutor and a member of the high school PTA.

Sadly, my marriage ended after almost twenty-five years, but I was lucky enough to meet my second husband, Howard, to whom I've been happily married for nineteen years. I became a stepmother to two children and we have lived in Glasgow since 1999. We now have eleven grandchildren between us! I did eventually take up studying again — first at the local high school and college and then with the Open University where I studied maths, gaining a degree after five years.

It was in Glasgow that I joined the only Reform synagogue in Scotland. One thing led to another, and I am now a regular service leader, a senior warden and an administrator at the synagogue.

My communal involvement has been much wider over the years. I went to my first Day Limmud in 2002, which I loved, and eventually became seriously involved as variously Secretary, Treasurer, Programme Coordinator and Chair of Limmud Scotland. This, in turn, led to my long-term involvement with the Scottish Jewish Archives Centre where I am currently a Trustee, Office Manager, Volunteer Coordinator, archivist and tour guide. I've also been part of a team which has just successfully created and launched the Scottish Jewish Heritage Centre. Along the way I have also been the Honorary Secretary and Vice President of the Glasgow Jewish Representative Council as well as Vice Chair and, currently, Honorary Secretary of the Scottish Council of Jewish Communities.

Being part of the small, distinct, lively, but sadly shrinking Scottish Jewish community poses its challenges but does engender a special feeling of solidarity and warmth — even if it occasionally feels a little claustrophobic! It does mean that a few people are called upon to step up to a number of roles, but that brings opportunities and a feeling that you're contributing in a meaningful way. I wouldn't want to live anywhere else...

I love my Jewishness, my family and friends. I'm increasingly aware of the Bundist contribution to Jewish radicalism; fascinated by the mythical / biblical constructions of Jewish history in the teeth of the evidence; yearn for pickled herring and *heimishe* gherkins; and thrive on Jewish jokes.

I was born a South African *Litvak* Jew but it was Israel, not my orthodox *bar mitzvah*, that made — and remade — my Jewishness.

I knew Jews were persecuted everywhere. I was aware of family lost in the Holocaust. But the religion offered me nothing. I felt uncomfortable in apartheid South Africa and found salvation, at fourteen, in a loose, ecumenically-Zionist social network called Young Israel.

It accommodated my atheism, taught me — an acutely shy young adult — to string words together in public, and gave me a sense of community as we sat huddled over short-wave radio cheering the troops on towards the Suez Canal. I loved Israel and was going to run away and join the Israeli army.

At eighteen I did indeed try a two-month winter leadership course in the promised land, but returned disquieted. My Israeli *chaverim* talked about "the Arabs" like blacks were talked of back home.

After a first degree at Wits, where I was involved in struggles against segregation, I went on to university in England in 1961, intending to return to fight apartheid. But I never went back; open political activity there was suppressed in my absence. Besides, I was now part of a bigger project, rejecting both Washington and Moscow for International Socialism and making the revolution in the industrial heartlands.

My residual Zionism didn't survive those triumphalist six days in 1967, which revealed an ugly face I hadn't noticed before. I turned ever more to my anti-capitalist internationalism, seeking other ways of making the revolution. I started Pluto Press, lectured, organised, occupied, was a trade-union militant, fostered political debate, demanded radical change. I drew universalist lessons from my Zionism: being Jewish was a struggle for justice for all; all peoples were chosen.

The second intifada reinvigorated my Jewishness. The not-in-my-name movement that rippled through Jewish communities around the world refashioned my politics. My late partner Irene Bruegel (d.2008) visited Palestine with Women in Black and saw the occupation at first hand. She galvanised me and others to launch Jews for Justice for Palestinians.

Today I express my Jewishness through Jewish Voice for Labour: for the many not the few. *L'Chaim!*

"Are there any Jews?" This was the first question my wife asked me nearly fifteen years ago when I was offered a teaching post in Scotland. I conducted online research and it appeared that Edinburgh was the new Jerusalem! However, upon arrival, we soon discovered that there were very few Jews actively engaged in Jewish communal affairs.

I often wonder why my Jewish roots are so deep and seem to deepen each day as I now approach the winter of my life. I suppose it begins with my father who was a first-generation American Jew whose parents escaped the pogroms to find a new life in Texas. My father, who had been a child during the Great Depression, was always very frugal. However, one day he came home from his hardware store and showed my sister and me four tickets for a new musical entitled *Fiddler on the Roof*. He told us to get dressed as he and Mama were taking us to the Music Hall. During the opening number, 'Tradition', Papa squeezed my ten-year-old hand and I looked up at him. He was quietly crying. He then turned to me and whispered, "That is my family."

Papa was once asked by a newspaper if he saw himself as an American or a Jew or both. He responded by saying that he was first a Jew because that is an identity that he would carry with him everywhere he went. He then said he was also a proud American. I suppose I feel the same way about Scotland.

In 2017 the Edinburgh Jewish community celebrated our 200th anniversary. That same year the Edinburgh International Festival celebrated its seventieth anniversary. I proposed to the leaders of the Edinburgh Jewish Cultural Centre that we erect a plaque in our city's main concert hall honouring the two Jewish founders of the festival (who were refugees of Nazi Germany) and also the 200th anniversary of the Jewish people in Edinburgh. They supported my request and I raised the funds for the large plaque that now resides just outside the Royal Box in the concert hall. Every time I see this plaque I am filled with pride as I recognise that a small group of people and two outstanding Jewish artists could help to dramatically improve my adopted country. Long may it continue and I look forward to playing a leading role!

In the picture I'm wearing my Netzer shirt. Netzer stands for *Noar Tzioni Reformi* — Young Reform Zionists. I'm involved in LJY, Liberal Jewish Youth, which is British and part of Netzer. I first went to summer camp with them when I was eight. I've had leadership training with them, been on an Israel tour and a Europe tour as well, summer camps, days out... It's made me who I am I guess.

I'm doing my A-levels at the moment and I'm planning on doing neuroscience at uni. Before that I want to take a gap year in Israel on this programme called *Shnat* which is run by Netzer.

It's a community that's always with you and it's global, which is nice. People all over the world would be able to recognise it. Once we were in Israel and some people from New Zealand recognised my top and that was really cool.

There's not a lot of Jews where I live but I don't feel isolated. Only one or two of my friends here are Jewish. The only Jewish friends I have are from camp and I only see them a few times a year. They all live round the country. My friends that aren't Jewish live nearer to me.

I define myself as a Liberal Jew. I share LJY's values, striving for equality — it's quite left-wing I guess. They teach you values but also to make up your own mind about it. I've been involved in Liberal synagogues most of my life. Usually I go every Saturday. I teach there and I put together lessons — next week's is on Passover.

My background's quite complicated. My Mum's Jewish, from Russia and Ukraine. My Dad's Nigerian and he was brought up Christian. They aren't together anymore. I once asked my Dad if I could learn his language but he said I was too busy learning Russian. I'm taking A-level Russian now. I went to Russia once when I was really small but I'd like to go again.

No one's ever said anything out loud but I could see how it could be surprising for some people that I'm Jewish. In the media Jews always look one way, with the big noses and stuff.

Sharon   Finchley

I am that Jew. The one who is completely Jewish, but at the same time a *yogini*.

I was born the same year apartheid was legalised, the same year Israel was recreated as the Jewish state. I grew up under the umbrella of Jabotinsky's revisionist Zionism, his portrait taking pride of place in the hearth of our home. My father had been his companion and friend, touring together around Southern Africa during two of Jabotinsky's several visits.

I am an immigrant. I arrived in the UK in 1969 aged twenty-one, sailing on the last ocean liner from South Africa. Intoxicated by the smell of freedom, I knew as soon as the boat docked in a foggy Southampton that I'd never return to the police state of my birth, where, aged five, I ran home from my first day at school to ask my mother who Jesus was and why I had killed him.

Growing up in Pretoria away from the hub of Jewish 'Joburg', my friends were not only from within the Jewish community, but from the broader multi-faith groups around me. I enjoyed life in the warmth of close-knit family where I learned to value life and respect for all fellow beings. I camped by bonfires, swam, hiked, played tennis and grew up somewhat of a tomboy, playing cricket and football as well.

This early influence set the course for my adulthood in which the dignity of man(kind), Jabotinsky's concept of *Hadar*, is central. Having established my home in London with my husband and two children, I worked as a radiographer in many hospitals whilst also embracing my yoga practice, qualifying as a teacher and yoga therapist. I learned in my studies that like Judaism, yoga shares a belief system with *kabbalah*.

I was fortunate to have discovered Iyengar yoga early on as it has proved to be the backbone of my life, providing me with a passion and stability as it became increasingly clear that the early heyday of freedom in the UK was being soiled by the resurgence of Jew hatred. The warning bells of Holocaust were beginning to sound again and I began to realise that Jews were once more becoming a target, I feared that I was unable to ensure the safety of my children. And so, in the mid-1990s, I became an activist for Jews and Israel in the knowledge that I'd never live in peace with myself if I simply watched without trying to make that difference.

And all the time my companion is my yoga, keeping me steady in my resolve and stable in balance to face an increasingly destabilised world.

I'm a Sephardi Jew. My ancestors were expelled from Spain in the fifteenth century and settled in Morocco. Jews weren't allowed to live in England until 1656. So when Gibraltar was taken over by the British in the eighteenth century, that meant Jews like my ancestors were able to come to the territory. My family was part of the Jewish community of Gibraltar. It still exists and has become very observant. Some of them came to England though and there is a Gibraltarian Jewish community in Hendon.

My parents stayed in Britain after much of the population was evacuated in the War. I grew up in Stepney in East London. My parents were observant, but not 'black hat' observant! Our community was Bevis Marks *shul*, which is Sephardi and has a long history. It's still my community although I mostly only attend services on the High Holy Days. I live in Hampstead now.

I became the manager of Bevis Marks twenty years ago. I basically ran the building and I am also responsible for the heritage and museum side of things. We've expanded and raised a lot of money to renovate the place. I never worked in a museum before that — I just fell into it — but now I am starting work on another museum project.

Helen   Oxford

I grew up in Australia among a family of Holocaust survivors originally from Poland, who found refuge in Melbourne after the war. Yiddish was my first language, the everyday language of my parents and the extended survivor family. *Shabbos* and Jewish festivals were marked in a very natural, traditional, folkish way with lots of chatting — in Yiddish.

At a very early age, an uncle began to teach me the Yiddish alphabet — one letter per day. I read and wrote Yiddish before English. I attended a Yiddish-speaking kindergarten, a Yiddish Sunday school and summer camps where Yiddish was an integral part of daily activities. By the time I was seventeen, I had completed a Yiddish teacher-training course and began to teach Yiddish.

As a child I was regularly taken to Yiddish cultural events: films, theatre productions, song recitals, recitations, lectures. I was later a member of the newly established Yiddish Youth Theatre.

After completing academic studies in music, English literature and then pedagogy, I decided to pursue higher academic studies in Yiddish in Jerusalem and then in Oxford.

A career which combines the love of one's own language and its vast literature with a passion for teaching and research is indeed a gift. For twenty-plus years I lectured in Yiddish at University College London, and prior to that I taught Yiddish language and literature for the Oxford Centre for Hebrew and Jewish Studies. I am also Director of the London Yiddish summer course Ot Azoy.

Whilst studying in Jerusalem, I worked as a research assistant for Prof. Dov Noy (1920–2013), a ground-breaking folklorist. My work focused on Yiddish folk materials. Each Monday, Dov and his archaeologist wife Tamar would host an open-house evening. Everyone was welcome. All shades of Jews and non-Jews attended representing multiple languages and cultures. Ashkenazi and Sephardi Jews, religious and secular. Israeli Arabs, Palestinians, Bedouin, Druze, Greek Orthodox, evangelical Christians. Amongst them were also some writers, academics, musicians, Holocaust survivors. Most importantly, people really talked and listened to each other.

Yiddish language and culture has never had geographical boundaries. Through it, I engage with Jewish tradition, history, culture and literature and its intersections with other cultures and lands. Yiddish and being Jewish is part of a life-long journey to try and understand my / our own history and culture and to explore multiple worlds and our shared humanity.

My family spans the spectrum of Jewish denominations: my parents are modern orthodox, one of my sisters is Haredi and my brother-in-law is a Reform / Masorti rabbi. My parents are religiously devout but politically they've always been quite progressive — particularly on Israel-Palestine — and this definitely informed my own politics as I got older.

I went to a modern orthodox primary school where Jewish studies was taught in Hebrew, and attended Bnei Akiva youth camps throughout my teenage years, eventually becoming a *madrich*. I spent my gap year studying in a religious Zionist *yeshivah* in Jerusalem — a fact that often surprises people who meet me now.

While I am no longer strictly observant or affiliated with any communal institutions, my Judaism remains a salient part of my identity, which, is expressed culturally, politically and through my values.

I co-founded the progressive Jewish media platform Vashti in 2019, in order to broaden discussions that were happening about the Labour Party, antisemitism and Israel-Palestine. We've since realised our purpose is much bigger: to cultivate a culture of the Jewish left and to connect it with the rich history of British Jewish radicalism that is gradually being forgotten.

I am also proud to have helped to found Na'amod, a movement of British Jews seeking to end communal support for Israel's occupation of the West Bank, East Jerusalem and Gaza. Na'amod takes inspiration from Jewish social justice traditions as well as from activists in the US and in Israel-Palestine who are also working to end support for the occupation in their respective communities.

Na'amod was also catalysed by a more local controversy that became known as 'Kaddish for Gaza', when Jewish activists recited the mourner's prayer in memory of Palestinians killed at the Gaza border in 2018. Our intention was simply to affirm the grievablity of Palestinian life and to challenge their dehumanisation by parts of the Jewish community. As if to illustrate our point for us, the Jewish communal mainstream reacted to this small gesture of solidarity with shock and fury. The Jewish press slandered us as terrorist sympathisers, an Orthodox Rabbi compared our actions to that of *kapos*, and pressure was placed on Jewish institutions to strip attendees of their communal positions.

At the time, I remember finding the ferocity of the criticism difficult to stomach, especially when it came from friends and acquaintances of mine. However it didn't dent my enthusiasm for anti-occupation activism.

Rachel

I was born in a village in the Carpathian Mountains, in what was then Czechoslovakia, very near the Romanian border. It's now in Ukraine.

I was just fourteen when I was taken to the camps, in 1944. The village was emptied out. My father was taken away as a forced labourer earlier, in 1942, and was never heard of again. We were taken to a ghetto and then to Auschwitz. I lost my mother and three of my siblings the day we arrived there. My brother Chaskel and I were separated but we survived. Then I was moved to another small camp, digging ditches. After that we were made to walk and I ended up in Belsen, to be liberated by the British.

My brother found me near Bratislava after the war. My uncle looked after us for a while. He eventually went to Palestine but he arranged for us to join a group of children who wanted to come to Britain. We ended up in Northern Ireland. My brother was found to have TB and he was shipped off to Kent so he could go to a sanatorium. He took a long time to get better but in the end he was able to leave and get married and have children. He died young though, at age forty-two.

In the end we settled in South London, at first in hostels and then a wonderful family took me in as a lodger. I stayed traditionally observant and I still am, but I'm not 'religious religious'. I joined the synagogue where I lived and the local Maccabi club, and that's where I met my husband. He was a mechanical engineer. We lived mostly in South London but for a while we lived in Copenhagen and in Nairobi. I worked as a dress-maker at a high class designer place in Bond Street, then when the kids were little I taught students dressmaking.

Now I'm in Jewish Care independent living accommodation. My daughter still lives in South London and my son and two grandchildren live in California. I'm still active. I go a survivor's centre regularly and I'm part of a group that speaks Yiddish together.

I've told my story many times. It took a long time to start and it was very difficult at first. I've been giving talks for years, at schools and other places, and it unsettles me every time.

I grew up in a Liberal Jewish household.

My mother grew up in a strict Catholic household and had already been exploring Judaism before she met my dad at university. She converted at the LJS (Liberal Jewish Synagogue), they got married at the LJS and Rabbi John Rayner did my baby blessing at the LJS.

My parents were really involved in our synagogue and I went to *cheder*, but what was most significant to me was growing up in ULPSNYC (Union of Liberal and Progressive Synagogues Network of Youth Clubs) which led to me doing *Shnat* in Israel when I was eighteen. At the end of that year I had a place at Cambridge and although I wanted to stay in Israel I felt the pressure to come back and take up the place. But after a year I still missed Israel so I went back. A lot of that was to do with exploring the idea of being Jewish 24/7. I wasn't particularly religious when I was in Israel — in fact I used to manage bars like Mike's Place in Jerusalem — but that was my Jewish identity.

I eventually went back to the UK to do a degree and my plan was to get an MBA and buy into Mike's Place. To pay my way I started teaching in synagogues and I became aware that there weren't that many young female rabbis around at the time as role models. That coincided with studying Jewish philosophy at Kings College which opened my mind to new ideas.

I started to train for the rabbinate at Leo Baeck College in 2003, when I was twenty-five. I loved it. I still had in the back of my mind the idea that I'd go back to Israel, but then in my penultimate year I was offered a job as rabbi at Kingston Liberal Synagogue.

Kingston was an amazing community for me. People don't move to places like that because of Jewish reasons. The synagogue is the sole source of their Jewish identity so the rabbi has to build a community that is religious, cultural, social — all those things.

Later on I became Chair of the Liberal Rabbinic Conference and it became important to me to be able to build Liberal Judaism as a movement. That's how I ended up in this job as Director of the Liberal Movement.

I was born with cerebral palsy and therefore I didn't walk or talk clearly till age seven or eight, however most people can understand me and my sense of humour. I was fortunate to attend mainstream school and achieved GCSEs and a BTEC that enabled me to gain a place at Leeds Metropolitan University to study computing, and I graduated with a BSc Hons. In 1996 I went to Israel for two years. In 1999 I started with Compaq on their graduate training programme in Warrington and lived in Manchester in the Jewish community for three years where I made a lot of friends. I wasn't exactly *frum* but it helped me on my way to becoming more religious.

Eventually I returned to London and started with Whizz Education in 2005 where I was a sales representative for twelve years and negotiated school contracts of over £1 million of business. Maths Whizz was an amazing piece of software and it would have been very beneficial for me at school as I always found maths really hard as due to my limited writing abilities it meant teachers could never see my working out. Technology is quite liberating and I have a passion for it. Without my Blackberry I'd be lost! I can't use an iPhone though as touch screens are quite cumbersome.

For *bar mitzvah* I read *maftir* and *haftarah* in Stanmore *shul*. In 2005 my parents moved to Hampstead and were instrumental in establishing The Village Shul, where I had the opportunity to read my *haftarah* again. The Rabbi challenged me to do more *haftarahs* — I've read about eight or nine new ones now. My family are very good and supportive and I know many people in my community, I'm always being invited for Shabbat meals. That doesn't mean that life has always been easy — it hasn't.

I am planning to make *aliyah* as Israel has always been a very important part of my life and I've always wanted to live there. I've always felt that Israelis understand disabilities a lot better than in the UK, probably because they are used to dealing with injured soldiers and understanding they can't patronise them. What I've achieved in my life is amazing but sometimes I need to acknowledge things I am finding difficult. I'm at the point now where I need a new challenge. My Hebrew isn't bad. I actually find it easier to talk in Hebrew than in English because there are fewer words!

Marianne

I have an unusually rich and varied life. I work as a rehab vet, helping dogs and cats to recover from orthopaedic and neurological conditions. My interests span science and art. In my spare time, you might find me comparing scientific studies, or out there sketching or painting or seeking new tunes, playing the violin or singing.

I live with my family in a Hertfordshire village, and we often go about as if we're not Jewish at all. However, there's always been a fine thread of Judaism weaving in and out of my life.

I grew up in Gants Hill, Ilford, a multicultural neighbourhood. We were active members of the Reform synagogue in Newbury Park. This is where my sister and I had our *bat mitzvahs* and where, years later, I got married — to a man who had also been a member of the same *shul*.

Since childhood, I have felt uneasy about going to religious services. I don't like being told to read things out if I don't fully believe in them or know the language. The grown-ups running the educational and social aspects of this *shul* made noble attempts to get me involved as a child but I did my best not to get too drawn in. However, I did sing in the youth choir: it was a decent introduction to ensemble music.

At Edinburgh University, I found myself to be the only Jew in my large year group at vet college. I went to a few Shabbat dinners with the university Jewish society in my first term but I soon realised that, for stimulating conversation and to make true friends, I needed to seek people who I particularly got on with rather than using religion to dictate my social life.

My remaining link with Judaism is through music. I took up klezmer about a decade ago. The genre feels very natural to me, and playing klezmer together feels uplifting. There's no written music, just a repertoire of traditional tunes that musicians can play around with together. I have since made many friends through playing at klezmer jams in London: many of these people are Jewish, but not all.

Along with a friend, I now perform music at Jewish care homes. We're known as Kleztopia. Having started as a klezmer duo, we added in Yiddish songs once people starting to ask for them. It is moving to see members of the audience singing along. Many of them talk to us afterwards and share stories of how their *bubbas* sang these same songs to them years ago. They ask us to come back soon and to keep going with the Yiddish: not to let the old language disappear.

My dad's side of the family come from the Caribbean. My mum's dad's side of the family was Jewish. He's not here no more and he never really used to speak about it. He had a weird accent. The place where I'm from doesn't really have any Jews. It's more Muslims on the estate.

This is my third time in prison. I was in segregation — we call it The Block — for about two months. My cousin passed away when I was in there and the Jewish chaplain here came to see me. She's a really good woman and has helped me a lot. She's like a mum. So I started going to the Jewish group here. I'm still learning the prayers, for the wine, for the bread, for the candles. I suffer from dyslexia and my brain's not so good at keeping memories.

This jail's okay, it's quiet and there's no violence. There's three of us on my wing that are Jewish. We look after each other. I don't get any hassle for being Jewish. Other jails are really bad. In Woodhill there's no way I would say I was Jewish; no chance.

There's been loads of stress in my life. My grandad's not here no more. My nan's got cancer. Too many things hit me at once. When I was about nine, my cousin passed away. That really hurt me. I was twelve when my brother got done for murder, he was only fifteen at the time. That changed me. It broke something inside me. After that I wasn't listening to no one, no one could control me. I was doing stupid stuff.

I was fifteen when I went to jail, for something I didn't do. I was on remand, got found not guilty and when I got out I told my girlfriend I wasn't going back to prison. But when I was nineteen I did, for GBH. I pleaded guilty, did fourteen months and promised my girlfriend again that I wasn't going back. But I was mixing with the wrong crowd and ended up coming back for GBH with Intent. And this is where I am now.

It's hard. I'm really lucky though as my parents are really supportive; I see them a lot. My cellmate hasn't had a visit or got letters since I've been in.

This jail has given me more hope than the others did. I'm working towards de-cat, stepping down to an open prison. I want a family and kids, that's the main thing I want. My girlfriend's left me now.

My cell's in the best wing here; it's all right. I like keeping my stuff clean. I like to look good. It gives me confidence. I have a shower in my cell and I use half a bottle of shampoo every day on my hair, and shampoo is really expensive in here! I work in the kitchens and I draw, listen to music, watch TV. I'm good at picturing things in my head and drawing them on paper. I work out too; there's a spinning class. But I can't really read and write. To be honest with you, I'm twenty-four and I'm embarrassed — at this age I should be able to read and write.

Since this photograph was taken, David has been released from prison.

I've lived in Stamford Hill all my life, aside from a few years in *yeshivah* in Israel and in Antwerp.

I am part of the Bobov Hassidic sect. Compared to some of the others it's quite neutral and non-specific in terms of its impact on everyday life. It's really about what *shul* I go to and travelling to the *rebbe* for *yom tov*. And the dress obviously. Our *payos* are not tucked in behind the ear; on *Shabbos* we wear a tall fur hat and white knee-high socks. But quite a lot of these things are shared by other Hassidic groups as well. Still, insiders would recognise the nuances.

I'm in branding and advertising. I always had a certain feel for that kind of thing. After I married, I was in *kollel* for a year or two. It started when a friend asked me to do a job for him and then I started getting more into it. I went onto Amazon and found a book on advertising which opened a whole new world for me. I was always a bookworm so I read everything I could get hold of and took a few online courses. I started learning about psychology and behavioural economics. Eventually I bought a business from a friend.

It's a tight-knit community, with certain norms. I want to raise my children the way I was raised. There's no contradiction between that and the path I chose. In my generation especially there are a lot of people in business and a lot of blue-collar workers like plumbers and electricians.

Some parts of the community are stricter than others. For example, my son's school doesn't want people to have smartphones unless it's for business. So I had to explain that to them that I only do what is necessary for me on the internet. I wouldn't want my kids to be engaged in it.

Working has always been the norm in the community. My mother worked as a nutritionist for the NHS. My father is in antiques and property, but as soon as he became successful, he ran his business from *kollel*.

We speak English and Yiddish at home. With friends I speak more Yiddish. But even when I speak in English I use Yiddish words — and it goes the other way round too.

Sanjoy
Edgware

From a very early age, I had always been a regular *shul*-goer. Unfortunately, as I went into my teenage years, the number of young people who attended the *shul* I went to in Glasgow declined as my peers 'graduated' following their *bar mitzvahs* and were rarely seen again. So, as I stuck it out and kept going, I found myself by far the youngest person in what had become a bit of an old man's club.

My mother was born in India, but her family was originally from the UK; and my father was born in India and was an Army officer for thirty-five years. My mother and I (my parents divorced when I was eight) initially lived in a small village just on the outside of Glasgow. We were the only observant Jewish family — and the only non-white family — in the village. People were incredibly kind and friendly, but walking the three miles to *shul* (and back) every Saturday morning and being the only kid from that area to attend the Jewish school in the city, did make me feel different. It was the same when we moved into the suburbs of Glasgow. While there were more Jewish families, the numbers that were observant were not great and I attended a school that, while very multi-cultural, wasn't a place where I fitted into any particular group of kids with ease. University was much the same. In fact I did a doctorate at a very small university in the middle of nowhere where I was the only Jewish student that was *shomer shabbat*.

The photo was taken in the new South Hampstead Synagogue. Moving to London in the late 1990s, I was dragged along to the *shul* by my flatmate. People were remarkably friendly. As a newcomer, I was taken at face value for what I was. Over the years, I kept on coming. I moved house a few times, but each time I tried to move closer to the *shul* building so it would be a quicker walk and I could attend more services.

Based on my background, I was asked to oversee security at the building and, as a result, got to know pretty much every member and regular attendee. The community is a remarkable and diverse collection of individuals, from different walks of life, backgrounds and places. I suppose that through the changes in my life over the last twenty-two years, the *shul* has been the one constant, even when I moved abroad, and now to Edgware.

I grew up in Manchester, being born less than ten years after my parents left Iran during the 1979 Revolution. In doing so they followed my father's uncle who moved in 1950, who in turn followed his uncle who arrived in Manchester in 1914. Family legend says that he came to see the mysterious 'Manchester' that was written on the boxes of fabric he would buy to sell in Kashan.

I grew up speaking Farsi at home and it's still the only way to really communicate with my grandmothers. Unfortunately, I rebuffed my parents attempts at teaching me how to read it, something that I regret — and am belatedly trying to fix — to this day! Being born in the diaspora I'm not as educated and experienced in the 2,700-year-old Iranian Jewish culture as I want to be.

Growing up I had two concurrent Jewish identities — one at home and one in the wider community. At home we were proud Iranian Jews, eating *tahdig*, *gondi*, and *ghormeh sabzi* on Shabbat. The wider Jewish community is Ashkenazi-dominated, and I became a part of all of that too; eating chicken soup, roast chicken, and *challah* at communal Shabbat dinners.

In Manchester we attended our nearest Sephardi synagogue, where I still feel most at home today. Unfortunately it is suffering the same fate as many regional synagogues and is slowly diminishing in size.

I studied at the University of Leeds where I was involved in the Jewish Society and wider student political life. Following on from my year as a sabbatical officer for my students' union, I worked for a Jewish communal organisation before falling into the civil service where I still work. I've been with my boyfriend for nearly six years.

Being a minority within the Jewish community, I struggle to find a space where I am fully represented, so I work to make that space through organisations like Limmud and Sephardi Voices UK. Limmud is a grassroots Jewish learning organisation where everyone has the opportunity to learn and teach on any topic of Jewish interest. Through my involvement with Limmud over the past few years I have helped to bring in more stories and culture of Jews from the Middle East and North Africa. Sephardi Voices UK helps to record the stories of Jews who have left their homes in the Middle East and North Africa so that they are never forgotten.

"A season is set for everything, a time for every experience under heaven...
a time for planting and a time for uprooting the planted." (Eccl. 3:2) When I
converted to Judaism, I realized that I had found a spiritual home. Our physical
address changes quite frequently but Judaism provides a stable point of
reference that I will always have. The transitions in life can be quite difficult and
not always easy to plan. As a child, I never thought I would leave my hometown,
never mind live in South Africa for several years and then eventually settle in
the UK. The feeling of uprootedness and the anxiety it stirs up is balanced by
the spiritual anchor I have found in Judaism.

One of the most unexpected things I have found about Judaism is that it
is so joyous. Shabbat encourages us to take a break on the weekend and spend
time with family and reach out to people. Judaism is a life-centred religion. We
are not pinning all our hopes on heaven and saving up all our good acts to secure
a place in it. We do the *mitzvot* not only to help others but because it benefits
ourselves as well. I can do something helpful for others and at that the same time,
it is good for me to be with other people. Hillel is quoted in *Ethics of the Fathers*
(2:5) as saying, "Holiness is not achieved in isolation" and warning, "Don't separate
yourself from the community." This resonates with a reflection by Rabbi Jack
Riemer that I first heard at one of York's services that asks, "Did we fill our days
with life or were they dull and empty?" Judaism has given me the realization that
there have been some years when I really could have done better, and I now strive
to fill my days with life; literally, with people.

I respect that Judaism does not claim to have a monopoly on truth. It is
also refreshing that Liberal Judaism does not have a dogmatic approach to the
afterlife. In Judaism it is acceptable to say we don't really know what will happen
when we die. The Liberal Jewish idea of autonomy is also important to me.
The idea that we can critically interpret the Torah and not have to accept all
of it literally, especially the hurtful parts, is quite important.

I grew up in Ilford in the 1960s and '70s, which was then the biggest community in Europe. My parents were from Hackney and met in Poalei Zion. They were cultural and traditional rather than pious, both involved in the community through, amongst other things, Bnai Brith and the League of Jewish Women. My father went on to be the financial representative of the local synagogue. They sent me to *cheder*, Zionist youth movements, Jewish cubs and clubs, and instilled in me the importance of communal service. Not that I am suggesting they are to blame, but I might be described as a serial *macher*!

Back in the 1980s, after a gap year in Israel with Bnei Akiva, as an undergraduate at LSE, I threw myself into student politics. I chaired my Labour Club, ran unsuccessfully for General Secretary of the student union and I was elected national chair of the Union of Jewish Students in 1985, a role I assumed on graduation. I attended most NUS conferences between September 1982 and March 1987. I have a bit of an addictive personality and, as a budding lawyer, I felt I needed a clean break and stayed away from any kind of political engagement until 2005, when I got sucked back into it by ex-Trot friends from my student days. My reinvolvement was akin to re-entry from outer space, hurtling to earth (or was it in reverse?), helping to found Engage to counter academic boycotts of Israel and then the London Jewish Forum to engage with the Mayor's office — the incumbent was one Ken Livingstone — for which trouble the *Jewish Chronicle* listed me the twenty-eighth most influential person in communal affairs.

And it's been downhill ever since. Indeed my trajectory could be taken to resemble that of the decline of the political class and public discourse in wider society. And yet here I am still *machering* away: lay chair of Labour Friends of Israel, a trustee of Aish and, in a break from communal affairs, a trustee of Reprieve (the leading anti-death row charity). For relaxation there is special time in *shul* or with the *minyan* at work — prayer gives me a chance to surrender to something ordered, contemplative and virtuous, and that's where my picture catches me.

Just looking at someone cannot encompass their essence, nor what resides in their heart. There is a depth in our lives that both includes and transcends our looks. You cannot assume to know the nuances of someone's Jewish identity simply by looking at them. Only they know how being Jewish feels and how Judaism impacts their life.

Likewise, with gender identity: we cannot know just by looking at someone how they identify and what this means to them. Nor can we make assumptions based on someone's name, voice or clothing.

Abraham is called *'ha'ivri'*, 'the Hebrew' (Gen.14:13). The root *'avar'* means 'to cross over', 'to pass over', 'to traverse'. Abraham was invited to journey beyond: to move from his birthplace, traversing physical boundaries.

Being an *'Ivri'* is making a transition, experiencing milestones and challenges along the way. It is about the life-evolving journeys of our people: searching, venturing forth, being enslaved, encountering the unknown, yearning for liberation, carrying hope and dealing with frustrations. It is about the resource and resilience needed to reach a better place — a dream becoming reality.

G-d tells Abraham *'lech lecha'* (Gen.12:1), often translated as 'go forth' and 'go out' and literally meaning 'go *toward you*' (toward himself). Life is also an inner journey: searching for and re-discovering our own essence: a moving towards oneself. Transition has been an inner search and discovery of my authentic self.

I cherish being a Liberal Jew, with an intersectionality of identities — as a rabbi, chaplain, transman, husband, son, brother, uncle, poet, survivor of sexual abuse and more! My chaplaincy involves accompanying people through changes and challenges in healthcare journeys, offering emotional and spiritual support at these times.

An inherent part of my Jewishness and humanity is valuing inclusivity and celebrating uniqueness. Rather than being fearful of difference it would be heartening to recognise the plethora of gifts and enrichment diversity can bring.

I use 'he' pronouns and think of myself in terms of 'they', reflecting a multiplicity of selves: being assigned female at birth, growing up as a child, teenager and adult socialised as a girl and womyn. I am a transman, acknowledging and holding all parts of me — they enable me to be the man I am. With the current backlash of transphobia, sensationalism and prejudice, just being a trans and non-binary person is being an activist — not exactly a stereotypical notion of activism!

My need for congruency became stronger than my fear about how other people might react and relate to me. I can't be who some people might want me to be, I can only strive to hold my integrity, fulfil my potential and be who I am. Being a Jewish transman is about saying to G-d *'hineini'*: 'Here I am', the very depths of me.

Paul

Mill Hill

I was born in South Africa and made *aliyah* to Israel aged fifteen, with my parents. We settled in Raanana. It was only when I joined the IDF that I became fully Israeli. The IDF is a great social equaliser, you become close to people from across the country and society. I served as a tank platoon officer for four and a half years.

I had a number of choices upon release from service. One of them was a career in the security services, but I chose a different route and jumped on the first flight to the UK to read law at Leeds University.

I qualified as a solicitor in the City and practiced law for a couple of years before eventually establishing my own business in strategic land promotion and planning. I buy and sell land. Originally I was set to return to Israel after university to practice law, but the commercial opportunities were greater in the UK. I got married after university and had three children, so my return to Israel will have to wait.

During the Gaza conflict in 2008 I felt hugely frustrated at how Israel was being misrepresented in the media and in government. I came to the conclusion that we in the UK should advocate publicly for Israel. I found a home within the Zionist Federation and served as chair for a number of years. I saw this work as a continuation of being a soldier, standing up and defending Israel no matter where you live.

At some point I will return to Israel. But, for now, with my wife, children and a business all in the UK, I will be a twentieth-century Jew, flying back and forth to *Eretz*!

Britain is home. Israel is home. I love South Africa but it's no longer my home. I served as chair of my synagogue. I recognise the importance of the community support system that we have, with the *shul* at the heart of that. We have 2000 members and 80% only attend three times a year, but even that connection is important to them. The *shul* has been good for us all, so it's important that we give something back.

Recently I took on the chairmanship of yet another Israel charity, Technion UK, another hugely important institution for the country. Soon I will start shedding some of these titles, but whilst I still have some time, I will devote my energy to strengthen the Jewish community, Israel and Zionism.

My father escaped Baghdad when he was a child and emigrated to Israel as a refugee in 1951. My DNA is embedded with classic Iraqi hallmarks — we are passionate, committed, and driven. Growing up in Chicago, I knew I was different from the Ashkenazi kids in my neighbourhood. My father instilled me with a focus and an identity; a feeling of responsibility for generations of Jews that came before us, an unflinching love for Israel and a commitment to leadership.

As a teen, I babysat for religious families, which ended up derailing my prestigious academic pathway. By eighteen, I decided to become observant and 'stray' from the designated roadmap of my life. I made this change for so many reasons, but I saw beauty, simplicity, and wholesomeness in an observant life. It hurt my father so much, I know he was disappointed and even though I don't regret doing it, I do regret the pain it caused him.

Shortly after I met my husband, we got married and moved to London via Leeds and Bristol, and we have seven children. As I had become observant mostly through Chabad, the open approach to Jewish identity, as espoused by the late Lubavitcher Rebbe, is one that resonates with me. I don't identify as a particular type of Jew; I identify simply as a Jew. I do not care for politics or hierarchy, nor do I have any patience for judgmentalism or free-hand interpretation in religion — which applies to both liberal and orthodox viewpoints.

After years of raising and home-schooling our children, I knew that I needed to pursue a career. I wanted an identity beyond being a Rabbi's wife, a mother and a religious figure. I charted my own career path whilst remaining true to my roots.

I am grateful to be a religious woman. There is so much in *halacha* that supports my individuality and personal freedom. There is a wealth of personal guidance and interpersonal wisdom in Pirkei Avot. Shabbat is a vital island in time that I crave at the end of a busy week, and keeping Kosher just keeps you innovative and creative in so many ways; most of all, I love wearing a *sheitel* because it confirms my belief that G-d expects discipline, but it can and should be adorned in beauty. Without these guidelines, I think my personal and professional life would be unfocused, untethered and lacking value.

Most people don't know how to identify me: "Well, she's *frum*, she wears a *sheitel*, but now she's jetting around the world, fighting some cause, raising money, getting involved in fintech", and so on. Let them keep guessing.

I've always been very good with my hands. I learned most of my trade from following tradesmen around the house. There are lots of Jewish men who are that way inclined and then go into the City or become a doctor. To actually take that step and become a plumber — that wasn't seen as a job for a Jewish boy.

I left school without any A-levels, then went to work in a ladieswear manufacturers for three years. Then I was a manufacturer of ties for thirteen years until 1990, when the company closed during the recession. With my redundancy money I bought a van and started a property maintenance company. In 1996 I went to college and qualified as a plumber.

I work almost exclusively in NW London. 99.9% of my clientele are Jewish. They trust a Jewish plumber and I know what they can and cannot do as far as plumbing is concerned. So when I make plumbing alterations I ensure they are Shabbat and *yom tov*-friendly. The toilet and basins have to be connected to the mains rather than a pump, for example. For Shabbatot in the winter you need an awful lot of hot water for baths and showers. In an Orthodox household everyone's coming home at two o'clock on Friday and they all want to get ready for Shabbat at four. You need the biggest water tank you can get.

I've lived here in Muswell Hill all my life and I grew up in my local *shul*. It's a United Synagogue, but I wasn't always orthodox-practising. Now I'm an orthodox Jew. You can count the number of orthodox-practising people in the *shul* on one hand!

It's a very warm *shul*. Very friendly. Informal. People who come are welcomed. It's very socially aware. I was on the board of management, then I became a warden for eleven years, and I still help with certain things, like organising daily *minyanim*.

We had two children. Our youngest died in 2015. She'd been ill with Ehlers-Danlos Syndrome for fifteen years and was twenty-seven years old. The community was very supportive. Our other daughter lives in Israel with her husband and five children. She's what you'd call Haredi, and lives in the West Bank in a settlement called Beitar Illit. We stay with them regularly. It's a Haredi community and we don't entirely conform, but they don't insist that we do and it works out fine.

Glossary

This glossary contains only terms directly referred to in the text, with a few additions to aid in understanding the glossary itself.

For some Hebrew or Yiddish words, there may be alternative transliterations used elsewhere, so readers may encounter the same term with a different spelling. Hebrew plurals are generally denoted by the suffixes -ot and -im.

Aish: Abbreviation of Aish HaTorah, an international orthodox Jewish organisation, best known for its outreach activities to less observant Jews.

Aliyah: Modern Hebrew term for 'ascent', used to describe Jewish immigration to Israel.

Ashkenazi: Jewish ethnic group descended from those Jews who lived in Central and Eastern Europe. While today the majority of British Jews are Ashkenazi, until the mid to late nineteenth century the core of the community was Sephardi.

Bar Mitzvah: ('Son of the commandment') The coming of age ceremony for Jewish young people that takes place at the age of thirteen, usually commemorated by being called to bless and read from the Torah scroll in synagogue; often followed by a party for friends and family. The female equivalent is known as a **Bat Mitzvah** and in most progressive synagogues is identical to the male ceremony. In most orthodox communities Bat Mitzvah usually does not include the blessing and reading of Torah and takes place at the age of twelve.

Bevis Marks: The oldest functioning synagogue in the UK, built in 1701 by the Spanish and Portuguese Jewish community and situated in the City of London.

Bnai Brith: ('Children of the covenant') International fraternal Jewish organisation, organised into lodges and concerned with philanthropy, welfare, and social activism.

Bnei Akiva: ('Children of Akiva') Orthodox Zionist youth group, with branches around the world.

Bubba: Yiddish term for grandmother.

Bund: The Jewish Labour Bund was a pre-World War Two secularist non-Zionist Jewish socialist party, various forms of which were based in Eastern Europe and throughout the Jewish Diaspora.

CE / BCE: Common Era / Before Common Era. Date suffixes used by Jews and others in preference to AD and BC.

Chabad: (Also spelled 'Habad', also referred to as 'Lubavitch' or 'Chabad-Lubavitch'.) An orthodox Jewish Hassidic dynasty, whose last leader, Menachem Mendel Schneerson (known as the 'Lubavitcher Rebbe' or simply 'The Rebbe'), transformed it in the post-war period into an organisation known for its outreach to non-observant Jews.

Challah: Platted loaf of bread traditionally eaten on Shabbat.

Chanukah: A winter festival commemorating the Jewish recovery and rededication of the Second Temple during the Maccabean revolt of the second century BCE.

Chazan: A singer who leads the synagogue congregation in prayer (sometimes also known as a cantor).

Chaver: Hebrew for 'friend' or 'comrade'.

Cheder: ('Room') Jewish pre-Bar Mitzvah level education. These days the term is primarily applied to Jewish supplementary schools held at synagogues on Sunday mornings or on weekday evenings.

Chutzpah: Yiddish term that loosely translates to 'guts' or 'audacity'.

Eretz: ('Land') Short for 'Eretz Yisrael' — the land of Israel.

Frum: Yiddish term for 'religious' in the sense of being pious and stringent in Jewish practice. Sometimes a synonym for 'orthodox'.

G-d: Some religious Jews follow the practice of never fully writing the divine name in order not to risk its desecration.

Hadar: Loosely translatable as the 'nobility' of every Jew. A central idea in the **Revisionist Zionism** of **Ze'ev Jabotinsky**.

Haftarah: Selections from the books of the Prophets, read on the Sabbath and festivals following the reading from the Torah.

Halacha: System of Jewish law, traditionally viewed as being given to Moses on Mount Sinai. Halacha consists of numerous **mitzvot**.

Haredi: ('One who trembles') Term used for orthodox Jews who are particularly stringent in practice and usually seek to minimise engagement in secular life with a degree of self-segregation. Sometimes referred to as ultra-orthodox or strictly orthodox.

Hassidism: (Also spelled 'Chassidism'.) Spiritual revival movement that arose in the eighteenth century in Eastern Europe. Hassidic Judaism is organised into a variety of sects that follow particular dynastic leaders.

Hava Nagilah: Israeli folk song, commonly sung at celebrations.

Heimishe: Yiddish term roughly meaning 'homely', applied to individuals, groups, objects and spaces that are, for Jews, particularly comfortable and 'ours'. Sometimes a synonym for orthodox or Haredi.

Hillel: Jewish religious leader (d. 10 CE), associated with one of the key schools in rabbinic thought. Much quoted in the **Talmud**.

IDF: Israel Defense Forces.

Jabotinsky, Ze'ev (1880–1940): Revisionist Zionist leader.

Kabbalah: The Jewish esoteric mystical tradition. From the twentieth century onward, elements of this tradition have been popularised both within and outside Judaism.

Kaddish: Prayer recited in Jewish services in a variety of versions. 'Mourners' Kaddish' is recited by the bereaved at funerals, during the year-long mourning period and on the anniversary of death.

Kapo: Prisoners assigned as supervisors in Nazi concentration camps. Sometimes used by Jews as a highly derogatory term for other Jews, signifying treachery.

Kibbutz: Originally a collective farm, organised on egalitarian principles, kibbutzim were an essential component of the Zionist settlement of what is now the state of Israel. Today, many kibbutzim have diversified into other industries and loosened their collective practices.

Klezmer: Yiddish term for a particular Jewish musical tradition deriving from Eastern and Central Europe.

Kol Nidrei: The opening service of the festival and fast day of Yom Kippur, taking place after sundown. Begins with the Aramaic prayer of the same name.

Kollel: See **Yeshiva**

Kosher: System of Jewish dietary laws, including methods of slaughter and supervision of manufactured goods.

L'Chaim: Hebrew for 'to life'. Used as a toast.

Leo Baeck College: British progressive Jewish rabbinic seminary.

Leyn: Yiddish term for chanting Torah according to traditional modes of cantillation.

Liberal: In the British context, Liberal Judaism refers to a particular progressive Jewish denomination, today closely related in practice and theology to **Reform Judaism** but with a distinctive history and tradition.

Limmud: Conference / learning festival, initially held residentially over the winter holidays in the UK, now expanded across the world and to Jewish communities across the UK.

Litvish / Litvak: ('Lithuanian') Term used by and for Jews from a Lithuanian background. Also used to refer to that part of the Haredi world that is not Hassidic. Lithuania was a stronghold of opposition to Chassidism in the eighteenth and nineteenth centuries. Today, the friction between these Haredi streams is much reduced, although Litvish Jews are known for a particular emphasis on rigorous study over spirituality.

LJS: The Liberal Jewish Synagogue. Situated in St John's Wood, London, it is the oldest synagogue affiliated to the Liberal Judaism denomination.

Lubavitcher Rebbe: See **Chabad**

Macher: Yiddish for 'doer' or 'fixer'. Term used for someone who is heavily involved in Jewish communal activities, particularly as a lay leader.

Machon: Short for '**Machon Le'Madrichei Chutz La'Aretz**' ('Institute for Foreign Leaders') Training institution in Jerusalem for young leaders in Diaspora Zionist youth movements.

Madrich: Modern Hebrew term for a leader, as applied to volunteer leaders in peer-led Zionist Jewish youth movements.

Maftir: The final section of the weekly Torah reading. Particularly in orthodox synagogues, the Maftir and the **Haftarah** are read by the person celebrating **Bar Mitzvah**.

Masorti: Denomination that is sometimes understood as part of progressive Judaism and sometimes as a form of orthodox Judaism with a more liberal sense of the flexibility of traditional Jewish law.

Menorah: The term for the seven-branched candelabrum that was used in the Jewish Temple in Jerusalem and which has subsequently become a commonly-used symbol of the Jewish people and religion. A nine-branched menorah is used on the festival of **Chanukah** and is also known as a *hanukkiah*. On each of the eight nights of the festival, one more candle is lit, with one further candle used to light the others.

Mensch: Literally 'man' in Yiddish, the term has come to take on connotations of a decent, ethical and honourable person.

Mezuzah: Case affixed to the doorpost of Jewish homes containing verses from Deuteronomy, hand-written on parchment.

Minyan: A quorum of ten adult Jewish men required to fulfil certain **mitzvot** in collective prayer. Outside of orthodoxy, women may be counted as part of a minyan or a minyan may not be required at all.

Mikvah: Ritual bath, used by orthodox Jewish women after menstruation and for other purposes by both men and women, including as part of the conversion process.

Mitzva: A commandment. Traditionally, Jewish law sets out a large number of such **mitzvot** and orthodox Jews are divinely bound to follow the system as a whole. The term is also sometimes used in the sense of a good deed or act of kindness.

Mizrachi: Jewish ethnic group descended from Jews living in the Middle East, parts of North Africa and Central Asia. The majority of Mizrachi Jews living in the Middle East and North Africa were expelled or pressured to leave following the establishment of the state of Israel in 1948.

Orthodox: Collective term for Jews who see themselves as bound by the system of Jewish law given to Moses on Mount Sinai. Within orthodoxy, those who believe that it is possible to adhere to the law while taking a full part in secular life are often known as **Modern Orthodox**, while Haredi Judaism is sceptical that such a reconciliation is possible.

Parasha: ('Portion') The weekly reading of the Torah. The entire Torah is read over the course of a year (or tri-annually in some progressive traditions).

Payos: (Also pronounced *payot.*) Sidelocks worn by Haredi and some Modern Orthodox Jewish men in observance of a biblical injunction against shaving the corners of one's head.

Pirkei Avot: ('Chapters of the Fathers', or sometimes translated as 'Ethics of the Fathers'.) Collection of ethical teachings. Part of the Mishnah, which is itself part of the **Talmud**.

Poalei Zion: ('Workers of Zion') Socialist Zionist movement. The UK branch was affiliated to the Labour Party from 1920 to 2004, when it was rebranded the Jewish Labour Movement. The Jewish Labour Movement remains affiliated to the Labour Party.

Progressive: Umbrella term sometimes used for forms of Judaism that do not hold, in whole or in part, with the tradition that Jewish law is divinely ordained and unchanging.

Rebbe: An honorific title, derived from the word rabbi, today applied to spiritual heads of particular Hassidic sects.

Reform: Form of progressive Judaism that first emerged in the nineteenth century in Germany and the US. Stresses the autonomy of individuals, the non-binding nature of Jewish law and the continual nature of divine revelation. In the UK, also the name for a particular denomination.

Revisionist Zionism: Current within Zionism, originally formulated by Ze'ev **Jabotinsky** in the 1930s, that advocated for an uncompromising form of Jewish nationalism, based on the goal of a territorially maximalist 'greater Israel'. Associated today with right-wing politics.

Sephardi: **Sephardim** are descended from those Jews who were expelled from the Iberian peninsula in the fifteenth century.

Shabbat: The Sabbath, which runs from Friday evening to Saturday evening. Traditionally marked by synagogue services, festive meals (particularly on Friday evening) and a prohibition on work.

Shabbos: Ashkenazi Hebrew pronunciation of Shabbat.

Sheitel: Wig worn by some married orthodox Jewish women in observance of the commandment to cover the hair. Other head coverings, such as headscarves and snoods may be used in preference to, or combined with, the sheitel.

Shnat: Derived from the Hebrew word for 'year', used on its own (or combined with the name of a youth movement) the term refers for a year-long leadership programme in Israel organised by a youth movement. All or part of it may be located at the **Machon**.

Shoah: Hebrew term for the Holocaust meaning 'destruction'.

Shomer Shabbat: A Jew who observes the traditional Jewish laws of Shabbat. It is sometimes used as a synonym for orthodox.

Shul: Yiddish term for synagogue.

Talmud: The written compilation of rabbinic teachings, that constitutes the principle source of Jewish law. Consists of two components, the *Mishnah*, compiled in the third century CE and the *Gemara*, compiled in the sixth century CE.

Tikkun Olam: ('Repairing the world') A concept in Judaism that has been used to refer both to a mystical process of spiritual development and of improving the condition of human society in the world. In recent decades, it has been an important concept in Jewish social activism, particularly within **Progressive** movements.

Torah: ('Teaching') Torah can refer specifically to the first five books of the Hebrew Bible, or more generally to the totality of traditional Jewish teachings and writings. Synagogues of all denominations will possess at least one hand-written Torah scroll.

Tzedakah: ('Righteousness') The term most commonly used to signify the ethical obligation towards the other, often manifested in forms of charity.

United Synagogue: The largest British Jewish denomination, broadly following a modern orthodox approach, although many members of congregations affiliated to the United Synagogue may not be orthodox in their practice and some rabbis may lean towards Haredi Judaism.

Yeshivah: An educational institution where religious texts, principally the **Talmud**, are studied. In the Haredi world, a yeshivah for married men is known as a **Kollel**.

Yiddish: Language traditionally spoken by Ashkenazi Jews, based on German with influences from Hebrew and Slavic languages. Usually written in Hebrew letters. Today it remains the vernacular for many Haredi Jews and is also being revived and learned by a new generation of speakers.

Yom Kippur: Day of atonement, consisting of a 25 hour fast and multiple synagogue services.

Yom Tov: Literally 'good day' in Hebrew. Term used to refer to Jewish festivals.